3 32

		DATE DUE	

MARY LEAKEY

IN SEARCH OF HUMAN BEGINNINGS

MARY
LEAKEY

IN SEARCH OF HUMAN BEGINNINGS

BY DEBORAH HEILIGMAN

ILLUSTRATED BY JANET HAMLIN

Scientific American BOOKS FOR YOUNG READERS   W. H. FREEMAN AND COMPANY ◆ NEW YORK

Book design by Debora Smith

Scientific American Books for Young Readers is an imprint of
W. H. Freeman and Company, 41 Madison Avenue
New York, New York 10010

Library of Congress Cataloging-in-Publication Data

Heiligman, Deborah.

Mary Leakey : in search of human beginnings / by Deborah Heiligman; illustrated by Janet Hamlin.

p. cm. — (Science Superstars)

Includes index.

Summary : Examines the life of the noted anthropologist and describes her discoveries digging for fossils of our ancestors in East Africa.

ISBN 0-7167-6612-4 (hardcover). — ISBN 0-7167-6613-2 (softcover)

1. Leakey, Mary D. (Mary Douglas) 1913—Juvenile literature. 2. Women anthropologists—Tanzania—Biography—Juvenile literature. 3. Women archaeologists—Tanzania—Biography—Juvenile literature. 4. Fossil man—Tanzania—Olduvai Gorge—Juvenile literature. 5. Olduvai Gorge (Tanzania)—Antiquities—Juvenile literature. [1. Leakey, Mary D. (Mary Douglas) 1913- . 2. Anthropologists. 3. Women—Biography. 4. Fossil man.] I. Hamlin, Janet, ill. II. Title. III. Series.

GN21.L372H45 1995

301'.092—dc20

[B]   95-18691

                                                                                               CIP

                                                                                                AC

Printed in the United States of America
10 9 8 7 6 5 4 3 2 1

**For Ponnie and Jerry Weiner,
with love and gratitude. D.H.**

CONTENTS

How I Wrote This Book

To write a biography, you have to be part detective, part treasure hunter, and part thief. But above all else, you have to be an archaeologist. To write about the life of Mary Leakey, I had to uncover her past. I had to sift through her life and sort out her artifacts. I had to decide which pieces were the most important and would be most helpful in telling her life story to people who have never met her. The question I kept asking myself as I researched and wrote this book was, How can I bring Mary Leakey alive for you?

First, I had to dig. The most important artifact I found was a book Mary Leakey herself wrote about her life. It is her autobiography, which is called *Disclosing the Past* (New York: Doubleday, 1984). I also read another book she wrote about the rock paintings in Kondoa, called *Africa's Vanishing Art* (New York: Doubleday, 1983).

I read many magazine articles about Mary Leakey, and books, magazine articles, and encyclopedia entries about the science of prehistory. They are too numerous to list here.

I also talked to people who worked with Mary Leakey. Phillip Tobias and I had a wonderful talk about Mary Leakey and Dear Boy while he was in the United States. Then we corresponded when he went back to South Africa. Paul Abell told me about finding the footprints at Laetoli. They both told me some wonderful stories about Mary Leakey, some of which made it into the book. (One of the frustrations in writing a book is that you have to leave some good stuff out!)

My friend James Shreeve took time out from writing his own book about Neanderthals to tell me what Olduvai Gorge looks like (he's been there) and how it formed. Finally, Roger Lewin, a famous science writer who has written books about this subject and knows Mary Leakey, read the manuscript. He caught some mistakes I made (phew!) and gave me some more insight into Mary.

So you see, although a writer spends an awful lot of time alone while she is writing a book, she does not write it alone!

My husband, Jonathan Weiner, a science writer, took time away from his book to read my drafts and to explain to me, among other things, potassium/argon dating. My son Aaron was my first reader. He gave me great advice, and made a particularly good suggestion that I am grateful for. Benjamin was too young to read the manuscript, but he listened to my dinner conversations and took great interest in helping me figure out the secret of Mary Leakey. He also helped with the title.

Just as Mary Leakey had a team that helped her do her work, I could not have written this book without my team. At the head of the team is my editor, Nancy Feresten, whose job it is to make me write the best book I possibly can. I can't imagine a better editor. I also have a team of fellow writers who support me and tell me "you can do it" when I don't think I can. Without them, I'd panic a lot more.

All of this said, any mistakes in the book are my responsibility. I hope there aren't too many!

I hope you enjoy this book.

Deborah Heiligman, 1995

INTRODUCTION

Under the hot African sun, a woman stoops down, her eye caught by a glint of white. Gently, she brushes aside some dirt. It is a fossil. It is the tooth of a creature who lived over a million years ago. This tooth and the creature it belonged to hold secrets, secrets of who we are and where we came from. Mary Leakey keeps digging.

We know what people were like one hundred, five hundred, one thousand years ago. We know what they ate, what clothes they wore, which gods they worshipped. We know this because they wrote about themselves and their lives, and we can read their history. But how do we know about people who lived before there was writing, in prehistoric times? And how can we find out about the creatures who came before true humans, those who are our earliest ancestors? How do we even know they existed?

There are still many mysteries about the beginnings of humankind. But much of what we do know, we know because of Mary Leakey. Mary Leakey is an archaeologist, a scientist who studies objects from the past to find out about ancient people. She has spent most of her life searching for the stories of our earliest ancestors. For most of those years, she was on her knees, her hands in African dirt, looking for fossils.

This is her story.

CHAPTER 1

Pieces of the Past

When Mary Leakey was born, she brought with her pieces of the past, passed on by her father and her mother and their ancestors. These pieces fit together to create talents and interests that led Mary to help uncover pieces of *our* past, the past of all humans.

In Mary's past were adventure, art, and archeology. Her grandfather had been a painter. Her father, Erskine Nicol, was also a painter. He lived an adventurous and roaming life, traveling all over the world, painting landscapes. He would stay at one place until he had painted all that he wanted to paint, and then move on. When his money was about to run out, he would return to London to sell his paintings. After making enough money to support himself, he would travel and paint again.

Erskine Nicol was also interested in history and archaeology. He liked to learn about the past by looking at the tools, pottery, weapons, and other artifacts of people who lived a long time ago. He especially loved the history of ancient Egypt, and was friends with Howard Carter, the famous archaeologist who was to discover King Tutankhamen's tomb.

Erskine Nicol was in Egypt, in fact, when he met a young woman named Cecilia Frere, who was traveling as the paid companion of a rich friend. Cecilia's great-great-grandfather was a man named John Frere.

In 1797, John Frere was in Suffolk, England, where he saw some men digging up clay to make bricks. Stopping to watch, Frere noticed pieces of flint, a very hard quartz, sparkling in the clay. He saw that these pieces of flint were pointed, with chips flaked from their sides to create the points. Next to these flints were bones, including a huge jawbone that looked like it was from a mastodon, an extinct animal related to modern elephants.

Frere reasoned that these pieces of flint were human artifacts made by people, not by nature. Because they were with the mastodon bones, he figured they had been made a *very* long time ago. He wrote about the tools and drew detailed pictures of them. His writing and drawings were published in a scientific journal. Most people ignored his findings. They thought the world had been made just a few thousand years ago, and that the first humans were just like modern humans.

Years later scientists realized that what John Frere had found were indeed stone tools; they were ancient hand axes. A hand ax, one of the first all-purpose tools, is not really an ax at all. Ancient people flaked off pieces of a stone to create a sharp edge or a point at one end. Scientists now think that a hand ax with a sharp edge was used for cutting and scraping, and that one with a point was used for stabbing and piercing the hide of an animal. John Frere had the genius to realize that the rocks he had found were shaped by humans for a purpose. He is now considered the father of prehistory.

Cecilia Frere was an amateur painter, and she was very interested in art. She and Erskine became friends and quickly fell in love. After they were married, they lived on a houseboat on the Nile River in Egypt. When Cecilia became pregnant, they went back to England.

Mary Douglas Nicol was born in London on February 6, 1913.

Erskine Nicol wanted to start traveling again soon after, but World War I broke out, which made travel too dangerous. So he and

Cecilia rented a small cottage at Hemingford Grey in Huntingdonshire, in the south of England. Mary's first memories are of that cottage—with its water pump and outside toilet, called an earth closet. As a small child, Mary was already an adventurer. She loved to explore on the nearby River Ouse in a punt boat, poking through the water lilies and marsh marigolds.

The Nicols also spent a lot of time in London, where they stayed with Mary's grandmother (Cecilia's mother) and Mary's three unmarried aunts, Mollie, Toudy, and Marty. Mary loved her aunts, and they adored—and spoiled—her. Although there was never enough money in the Frere house, it was a very happy place to be. One Christmas, the aunts surprised and delighted Mary with a beautiful doll for whom they had made six gorgeous dresses.

Even though she loved to dress up her doll, Mary herself hated to get dressed up. Her usual outfit was a linen smock with large pockets, good for holding lots of treasures. She never got to like dressing up, not even as a grown-up.

It was in the house in London that Mary got to know her first dog. Jock, a smooth-haired fox terrier, followed her baby carriage to the park when her mother took her for a walk. Dogs weren't allowed inside the park, but Jock would always be waiting for her at the gate for the walk back. From then on, Mary found animals to adopt wherever she traveled. And travel she did, for World War I ended in 1918, when Mary was five. Soon Erskine Nicol was on the road again, his family with him.

CHAPTER 2

An Adventure Growing Up

Each autumn, the Nicols would take a boat from England to the continent of Europe. There they would catch a train to Italy or Switzerland or southern France. Mary was a great traveler, learning to sleep on a "bed" made out of train seats and suitcases.

Not all of Mary's adventures were pleasant. In fact, on her first trips, to Italy, she had an awful time. There was an earthquake, which terrified her. Then, on a family picnic by a river, Mary saw some boys pulling the legs off live frogs just for fun. She frantically tried to stop the boys, but they ignored her and her angry parents.

There was one good thing about Italy—the food. Mary especially loved Italian ice cream, and she loved fresh Italian cherries. But either the ice cream or the cherries gave Mary dysentery, a painful and dangerous infection of the intestines. She almost died.

Fortunately for Mary, her family traveled mainly in France, where she was very happy. It was in France that she first discovered archaeology. When Mary was about ten, she and her parents visited a museum of prehistory and became friends with the head of the museum, who was an archaeologist. It was there at the museum that Mary saw her first flint tools, harpoons, and bone points that had been shaped and

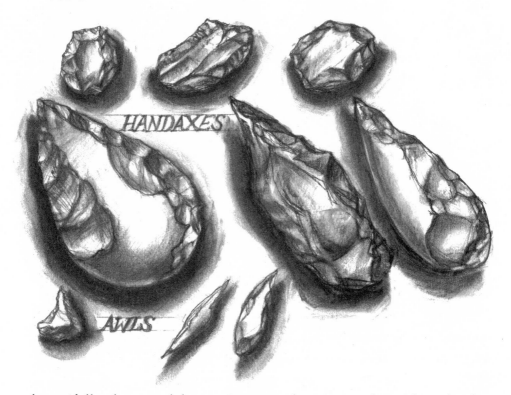

beautifully decorated by ancient people. It was there that she first learned about the Stone Age, which began about two and a half million years ago, when our human ancestors first made tools out of stones, and ended about five thousand years ago, when people began using metal.

The archaeologist also took Mary and her family to his dig, the excavation site where he was searching for artifacts of prehistoric humans. Today, archaeologists are very careful to sift through every speck of dirt when they are looking for artifacts and fossils (due in part to the work Mary did when she grew up!). But back then, the archaeologist and his helpers would just pick out the most interesting-looking pieces and dump the rest of the dirt and artifacts down the riverbank.

Mary and her father were allowed to search through the rejected dirt. They found many treasures, including ancient stone tools such as chisels and scrapers.

Erskine started a collection of their finds, but soon Mary took over. She made up her own classification system to sort the objects. She put together tools that looked the same—scrapers with scrapers, flint blades with flint blades, and so on. She wondered how old the tools were, and who had made them.

Two years in a row, Mary and her parents visited a village called Cabrerets, in southwestern France. There they made friends with the parish priest, the Abbé Lemozi. An amateur archaeologist, he taught Mary how to dig for fossils and artifacts. Once he took Mary and her mother to a cave called Pêch-Merle that had been discovered a few years before but was not yet open to the public. Mary's father stayed behind, probably because he was too large to fit into the small cave opening and passageways.

Mary, Cecilia, and the Abbé crawled through low and narrow passages, holding lamps to light the way. Mary's mother hit her head and it bled, but they kept going.

When they got into the cave itself, which was quite large, Mary saw paintings made by people thousands and thousands of years ago. She saw a pair of spotted horses. The head of the horse on the right was painted to fit onto a piece of rock shaped like the head of a horse. Around the horses were the silhouettes of five hands. There was also an engraving of a long, narrow fish, and a painting of a man impaled by lances. Looking up, Mary saw mysterious red dots that had been painted on the ceiling. Since the cave had not yet been open to the public, Mary was one of the first people in modern times to see these paintings made in the Stone Age. The Abbé explained that scientists could tell approximately how old the paintings were by what the artists had painted. For example, in one cave, there was an engraving of a mammoth that had been extinct for at least ten thousand years, so scientists knew that the art had to be at least that old. They could also date the art with tools and fossils found in the caves and by figuring out what the artists used to make the paintings and engravings. Later, scientists figured out even more precise ways of dating the paintings.

Years later Mary said that after seeing the cave paintings and learning how to dig for fossils, "I don't think I ever really wanted to do anything else."

When we look at the artifacts of Mary's childhood, we do not find report cards or class pictures or field trip permission slips. Although Mary was learning firsthand what most children could only read about, she did not go to school. Her father taught her to read when she was about seven or eight in Italy, and she learned very quickly. In France he tried to teach her some math, but he was not quite as successful. Mary also taught herself to draw, at the age of ten, and she was very good at that. But mostly Mary explored the limestone hills, the gorges, and the seashore, either by herself or with a friend.

Perhaps because he had not been so successful in teaching her math, Erskine hired a governess when Mary was twelve to teach her Latin, history, and other subjects. Mary hated the teacher from the be-

ginning. She found her ugly and awkward, and her hands were bright red. But worst of all, she was way too serious. A friend of Mary's nicknamed her the Uncooked Dumpling. Mary and her friend gave the Uncooked Dumpling a very hard time, and she finally quit. Erskine didn't try to hire a teacher again.

Erskine was Mary's favorite person in the world. He was a large, tall man with gray hair, a beard, and a long moustache. He dressed in shabby, paint-spattered clothes—as messy and old as Cecilia would let him get away with. He was interested in many things—people, history, flowers—and he loved to share those interests with Mary.

Every afternoon when Erskine was done painting, he and Mary would go exploring together. And every evening after dinner, Mary listened to the fascinating conversations he had with Cecilia and their friends.

Then, all of a sudden, when Mary was thirteen, Erskine got very sick. It was cancer. As her mother sat by his bed and the Abbé gave her father shots of morphine to lessen the pain, Mary went for walks by herself on the *causse*, the limestone plateau. Sometimes she went at dawn so she could see wild foxes playing and catch a glimpse of a rare wild boar. The animals gave her some comfort.

Very soon Erskine Nicol was dead. Mary and her mother headed back to England. There they would have to figure out how to live together without Erskine. And Mary would have to figure out how to finish growing up.

CHAPTER 3

"A Bit of a Bang"

With Erskine gone, it was painfully clear how different Mary was from Cecilia. Cecilia had been brought up to be a "lady," and she thought that since Mary was no longer a young child she should learn the "proper" way of acting and dressing. Mary fought her every step of the way.

Cecilia decided that Mary should go to school—and not just any school, but a strict Catholic convent school where the girls had to be quiet and well-behaved, and where they had to follow all the rules. Mary hated it! She didn't like the nuns, she didn't make any friends, and she didn't think she was learning anything useful. One day she hid in the boiler room so she didn't have to go to poetry class. Her punishment was to recite poetry in front of the whole school. When Mary refused, she was expelled from school.

Cecilia tried again, with another strict Catholic school. Mary did not like this school either. One day she pretended she was having a fit in the middle of class. She chewed soap to make it look as if she was foaming at the mouth.

Another day she created an explosion in chemistry class. It made a loud bang, and all the nuns came running. Mary was quite proud that

she had learned enough chemistry to create an explosion, but the nuns were not so pleased. Mary was expelled from that school too, and her mother did not send her to school again. "At least," Mary says, "I ended my school career with a bit of a bang."

Except for school, Mary adjusted well to her new life. She had her first garden, and two dogs: an Alsatian named Drago and a black cocker spaniel called Fussy. Drago was a vicious dog but very loyal. He seemed to take Mary's side against her mother—he wouldn't let Cecilia into Mary's bedroom! Drago soon went to live with the aunts, and Mary got a new dog to replace him: Jorrocks, a Dalmatian. Dalmatians became Mary's favorite dogs, and after that she almost always had at least one.

Mary was still very interested in archaeology and history. She continued to collect artifacts, but now she wanted to know more about the ancient people who had made them. She asked her mother to take her to Stonehenge, a famous prehistoric ruin on the Salisbury Plain in southwestern England. As she walked up to the circle of stone pillars, she felt like an intruder on an ancient landscape. With awe, she won-

dered, How did these huge stones get here? And who put them in this circle?

On the way back from Stonehenge they stopped at another stone circle at the village of Avebury. Since there was a small hotel in the village, Mary and her mother went back the next summer for vacation. There was an archaeological dig going on at nearby Windmill Hill. Mary's mother wrote a note to the man in charge, asking if they could come visit the dig. When they went, Mary met a famous archaeologist named Dorothy Liddell. Meeting her made Mary realize that a woman could be an archaeologist—and she knew that was what she wanted to be. But how?

Cecilia spoke to a famous professor at Oxford University to see if Mary could enroll there, even though she had so little schooling. The answer was no, she could not. How was Mary going to become an archaeologist?

When they got home, Cecilia and Mary moved from the suburb of Wimbledon back into London, where Cecilia could walk to visit her sisters and mother and Mary could easily go to universities and museums to hear lectures in archaeology, history, and other subjects. This was just right for Mary; she could design her own education and study just what she wanted. She went to many lectures and learned as much as she could. When Mary really wanted something, she went after it!

In her spare time, Mary rode horses and became a glider pilot. Gliding was dangerous, and Mary loved it. The glider, a simple airplane with no engine, was launched from the edge of a cliff using a heavy rubber rope called a bungee. A group of people would all pull back on the bungee until it was really tight—and then, snap, let it go like a slingshot. The glider would be catapulted into the air, and the pilot, as Mary says, "then simply stayed aloft as long as possible and landed somewhere convenient, when hopefully a car would arrive to tow the glider back to base." Mary got two certificates for reaching two levels of skill, but when she tried to get her third certificate, she crashed. Not to be discouraged, she named a new Dalmatian Bungey!

By the time Mary was seventeen, she had learned a lot about archaeology, and she was ready to do some excavating herself. She sent out letters to archaeologists asking to join them on their digs. Everybody said no. She sent more letters. Finally, somebody said yes. That somebody was Dorothy Liddell!

Mary worked with Dorothy Liddell for three summers at Hembury, an important late Stone Age site in Devon, England. Hembury is an ancient causewayed camp—made up of circular ditches, one around the other, broken up by ramps, or causeways. Why did Stone Age people create these camps? That is what Dorothy Liddell and her helpers wanted to know. When causewayed camps were first found, archaeologists thought they had been used as forts. But as they found pottery, flint axes, and other artifacts, the archaeologists began to see Hembury and other such sites as places where ancient people gathered for social activities and perhaps religious ceremonies.

Mary loved working at Hembury. It was a beautiful place, and it was exciting to help uncover the cobbled causeways and to find the ancient pottery and stone tools.

She also got a chance to put her artistic talent to work. Dorothy Liddell knew Mary was an excellent artist, so she hired her to draw some of their finds. During the winters, in the tradition of her great-great-great grandfather, John Frere, Mary drew ancient stone tools.

Gertrude Caton-Thompson, another famous archaeologist, admired Mary's drawings and asked her to draw pictures of some stone tools she had found in Fayoum, Egypt. She was so pleased with Mary's work that she invited her to come to an important lecture and dinner at the Royal Anthropological Institute in London.

That night would change Mary's life.

CHAPTER 4

The Mingling of Artifacts

If we could look at the evidence of Mary's life when she was twenty, we might find these artifacts: some lecture notes; khaki coveralls worn at the Hembury dig; drawings of Stone Age hand axes, anvils, and scrapers; and a matchbook from a dinner in 1933. Then we would begin to find artifacts from another person starting to mingle with Mary's—artifacts from a man named Louis Leakey.

Born in 1903, Louis Leakey was ten years older than Mary Nicol. He had grown up in Kenya, a country in East Africa. His parents were English missionaries who were in Africa to convert the Kikuyu people to Christianity. Louis adopted many of the ways of the Kikuyus and, at the age of thirteen, was initiated into the Kikuyu tribe in a secret ceremony.

By then Louis was already interested in prehistory. At age twelve he had been given a book called *Days Before History*. The book described stone tools and flint arrowheads used by prehistoric people in Britain. Louis started looking for prehistoric artifacts around his home in Kenya.

He did not find any flint tools, because there is no flint in East Africa. But he did find some pieces of a volcanic rock called obsidian.

These pieces had sharp edges and points, so they looked like tools to him.

His parents didn't think he had found tools, just rocks formed by nature. His Kikuyu friends told him the sharp stones were razors thrown down by the spirits of the sky. But Louis showed the obsidian to an expert at the Nairobi Museum, who told him he was right.

Only four years earlier, two American archaeologists had come to Kenya looking for Stone Age tools, but they hadn't found any. They had made the mistake of looking only for flint. Louis had recognized tools the grown-up scientists had missed! His expert friend told him to keep a careful record of his finds, which he did. So, like Mary, he began his career with stone tools.

When he was thirteen Louis decided that he would find out if Charles Darwin was right in thinking human beings had evolved from apes. Louis thought he would find evidence right there in Africa. Although most scientists of that time thought that people began in Europe or Asia, Louis was convinced that the journey of human evolution had begun in his homeland.

By 1933, when he gave his lecture at the Royal Anthropological Institute in London, Louis Leakey was already a well-known archaeologist and paleoanthropologist (a scientist who studies human ancestors).

Mary almost didn't go that night, because she thought "it sounded like a very stuffy affair." But she had never been to Africa, and she was eager to meet Louis Leakey and hear about his work there. She was especially interested in a remote spot called Olduvai Gorge, where Leakey had found some early Stone Age fossils. So Mary accepted Dr. Caton-Thompson's invitation and went to the lecture. Dr. Caton-Thompson even arranged for her to sit next to Louis Leakey at the dinner afterward. She knew that Mary and Louis would have a lot to talk about.

Mary liked Louis very much and was surprised that, even though there were important archaeologists at the table, Louis talked mostly to her. She was very pleased when he asked her to draw pictures for a book he was writing called *Adam's Ancestors*.

While Mary was working on those drawings, she and Louis became good friends. Soon they were more than friends; they had fallen in love. As nice as that sounds, it was very difficult because Louis Leakey was already married. He was unhappy in his marriage, but he had one child and his wife was pregnant with their second.

Many people were angry at Louis and Mary, including Dr. Caton-Thompson and Mary's mother. Cecilia was upset that Louis was married, and she didn't like him at all. Louis was a handsome, dashing, and charming older man, and she didn't trust him with her serious young daughter.

As usual, Mary ignored her mother's advice and kept seeing Louis. She also kept working, and her career really took off—not be-

cause of Louis, but because of her own hard work and perseverance. In 1934, at the age of twenty-one, she was in charge of her own excavation, at a site called Jaywick, near Clacton, in southeastern England. She worked alongside a leading geologist named Kenneth Oakley, and with him she wrote her first scientific paper. (Kenneth Oakley went on to become famous for uncovering an archaeological hoax called the Piltdown Man.)

In October of 1934, Louis went back to Africa. After hearing so much about it from him, Mary really wanted to go to Africa, too, especially to Olduvai Gorge. Mary promised to meet Louis in Tanganyika (now part of Tanzania) so he could take her there.

But Cecilia Nicol had other ideas. She hoped that once Louis left England, Mary would forget about him. She decided to take Mary on a tour of prehistoric sites in South Africa and Southern Rhodesia (now Zimbabwe). She figured that would satisfy Mary's craving for Africa and take her mind off Louis. Then they would go back to England together. Mary, however, figured that from Rhodesia it would be an easy trip to Tanganyika. Guess who won? In April, Cecilia went back to London in tears, and Mary went on to Tanganyika.

CHAPTER 5

Into Africa

Where was Mary heading on her journey? She was going to a place far from any town or city, a place that was a treasure trove for archaeologists and paleoanthropologists.

Back in 1911, a German entomologist named Wilhelm Kattwinkel was hunting butterflies on the Serengeti Plain in Tanganyika, East Africa. He was so caught up chasing a rare butterfly that he ran right to the edge of a very deep gorge. Some say he fell into the gorge; others say he almost fell and then walked down the steep slope. In any case, he stumbled onto something very exciting: a place called Olduvai.

Olduvai is the local Masai people's name for "place of the wild sisal." Growing in the gorge is a lot of sisal, a plant that is used to make rope. And hiding in the gorge are a lot of fossils, preserved through the ages by a lucky series of geological events—volcanoes erupting, earth shifting, rivers forming—that changed the shape of the land.

By looking at the rocks and the animal and plant remains, scientists have come up with a good idea of how Olduvai Gorge was formed. A few million years ago, Olduvai was a flat, wooded plain. It was a beautiful, tranquil place, filled with green grass, plants, trees, and herds of animals. Among those animals were rhinoceroses, elephants, lions, and apelike creatures. On the plain was a shallow lake where the animals came to drink and predators came to attack their prey. To the east of the lake were volcanoes. Every once in a while a volcano would erupt. Volcanic ash spewed onto the plain, covering the grass, the plants, the lake, and many animals. After some years, the grass would grow again, the lake would refill, and new animals would come to drink and hunt. Then another volcano would erupt, and spew more ash, covering the plain again.

About half a million years ago, the earth shifted, forming a depression in the land. So now there was a slope going down into the lake basin. The wet season brought day after day of pouring rain. During these rains, rivulets formed, then streams, then a river, cutting a gorge into the plain.

Nowadays, there are steep cliffs around the gorge, some as high as three hundred feet. As more rains fall the water washes off the surface of the cliffs and ground. It uncovers the bones that were preserved and buried by volcanic ash so many years before. Each year new treasures emerge, ready to be discovered.

Professor Kattwinkel returned to Olduvai two years after he had first stumbled into it, taking along a geologist named Hans Reck. At Olduvai, Reck found many fossil bones from prehistoric animals. He also found a human skeleton about seventeen thousand years old.

Years later when Louis Leakey heard about Reck's expedition, he had a feeling about Olduvai. Louis thought Olduvai would help him prove that our earliest ancestors came from Africa. He bet Reck that he would find stone tools in Olduvai. They went together in 1931, and within hours of reaching Olduvai, Louis found prehistoric stone tools that had been buried in the volcanic ash. Louis was thrilled. He thought that where he found prehistoric stone tools, he would also find evidence of early human ancestors.

THE HISTORY OF OLDUVAI GORGE

Olduvai Gorge a few million years ago.

A volcano erupts. Ash pours down.

Animals, trees, even the lake are buried in ash.
Stages 2 and 3 happen over and over again.

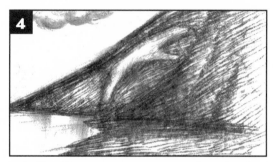

A half million years ago—an earthquake changes
the flat plain into a hill. The bones shift too.

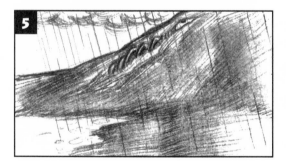

Rain washes soil down into the lake.

Bones lie exposed.

An archaeologist finds the bones sticking out of the ground.

In 1935 Mary couldn't wait to get to Olduvai Gorge. She hoped to find very old stone tools and maybe even fossil bones of early human ancestors themselves. After she left her mother in South Africa, she flew to Moshi, Tanganyika. Although she had been in Africa for a few months, she still didn't know what to expect. She was now heading into the wilds of Tanganyika, and it was the rainy season.

She soon learned that the pouring rains made travel very difficult. When she arrived at the airport, Louis was not there to meet her. She was advised to go to a hotel and wait. Alone in Africa, she hoped that

Louis would arrive soon. Sure enough, he walked in as she was eating breakfast the next morning. But the hardest part of the trip was yet to come.

To get to the Serengeti Plain and Olduvai Gorge, Mary and Louis had to travel up the side of an old volcano called Ngorongoro. The heavy rain had turned the dirt road into sticky, black goop, which was practically impossible to drive in. It took them two and a half days in the pouring rain to push the car sixteen miles up the volcano.

But what a view when they got to the top! Mary saw elephants, buffaloes, rhinoceroses, giraffes, wildebeests, and zebras grazing on the fresh green grass of the Serengeti Plain. Perhaps it was at that moment that Africa cast its spell on Mary. "Once you've been there," says a scientist who worked with Mary Leakey, "you fall in love with the place."

On the other side of Ngorongoro is the road to Olduvai Gorge itself. Olduvai was everything Mary had hoped for as an archaeologist. The gorge is like a layer cake that has been bounced around a bit, with fossils of different ages buried in different layers. You can actually *see* the layers, too, because they are different colors, made up of different rocks. One layer is reddish. Two others, the layers with the most fossils, are different shades of gray. It is the perfect place to hunt for fossils—if you know how, and if you are willing to work hard.

Mary and Louis pitched a tent halfway down a gentle slope in the gorge. During the day they explored a part of Olduvai called the Side Gorge inch by inch, sifting through the dirt. They started out very early in the morning, taking water bottles, and they stayed out until three or four in the afternoon.

Mary found fragments of a *Homo erectus* skull about one and a half million years old. *Homo erectus* is a direct ancestor of human beings. At the time that Mary found this skull, scientists thought *Homo erectus* was the first primate to be bipedal—to walk on two feet all of the time.

After Mary found the fossil, Louis named that site after her:

MNK, for Mary Nicol Korongo (korongo means "gully" in the Swahili language). They also found stone hand axes lying nearby. By the end of their three months at Olduvai, they had found thirty sites with fossils. Eventually there would be 127.

Although they had arrived at Olduvai during the rainy season, the rains soon ended. The river in the gorge dried up. The closest fresh water was thirty miles away. When the water they had brought with them was gone, they had to drink from what was left of the river—a series of stagnant puddles filled with rhinoceros urine! They filtered the water through charcoal, boiled it, and used it in tea with lemon, but they could not get rid of the taste of the urine.

Finally, it rained. Mary, Louis, and their assistants rushed to gather the water that had collected in the hollows of the tent canvasses. They drank it right up, forgetting that the tents had been heavily sprayed with insecticide. They all got violently ill; fortunately nobody died. They soon went back to work.

Since most of the time you're not finding anything, the work of looking for fossils can be tedious and tiring—and hot. (Imagine sitting on a beach in the hot sun, sifting through sand hour after hour and not going into the water at all.) But for Mary, Africa itself made up for the boredom. At night, as she lay in her canvas tent, Mary could hear lions and hyenas fighting over a kill. By day there were lions too. Once she almost tripped over a sleeping lioness. Fortunately the lioness was not protecting any cubs; if she had been, the story would end right here! Another time, while walking up a narrow stream, she ran right into a rhinoceros—head-on.

Being out in the middle of the Serengeti Plain, there were, of course, no stores where they could buy food. The team had brought with them canned sardines, rice, and jam, but Louis also killed gazelles so they would have meat. Mary didn't like the idea of killing the gazelles, and she didn't like the way the meat tasted. "But," she says, "I was not prepared to be thought 'soft,' so I made myself eat it without complaining."

At one point during this first stay at Olduvai, Mary and Louis were stranded with hardly any supplies. Their truck was a week late coming back with food, water, and cigarettes. (Mary and Louis were both heavy smokers.) So they set off in their car to find it. Over the border in Kenya, Louis accidentally drove off the road. The car got stuck deep in a gully. Since it was dusk, they camped out for the night next to the car. The next day, while local Masai warriors watched in amusement, Mary and Louis began to dig the car out with the only tools they had: two kitchen knives and two plates. (Because of their high place in society, it is beneath the dignity of Masai warriors to do

that kind of labor.) After digging all day, they finally finished, and guess what came down the road just then? Their truck, complete with shovels and towing ropes—and the supplies.

That season at Olduvai, Mary and Louis ran a medical clinic for the Masai people, as they would do ever after. Mary learned from Louis, who had done this before, how to treat everything from spear wounds to malaria. She bandaged wounds, applied medicines, and gave pills.

Some of the Masai came just to talk to Louis and to see the fossils. One day one of the men told Louis of another place that had "bones like stone." The man walked thirty miles and brought back fossil bones and teeth. Louis and Mary went to this place, called Laetoli, to see for themselves. They found some fossils, though none as interesting as those they had found at Olduvai. But Mary had a hunch that there was more at Laetoli and that they just had missed it. It would be forty years before Mary would go back—and find the secret of Laetoli.

At the end of Mary's first trip to East Africa, she knew she would marry Louis and spend her life in Africa hunting for fossils. Louis divorced his first wife, Frida, and on Christmas Eve, 1936, in London, Mary and Louis were married. Cecilia and Aunt Mollie were at the small wedding, neither of them happy about it. Three weeks later, Mary and Louis went back to Africa, this time for good.

CHAPTER 6

A Long Road

The road to scientific success was just as steep and difficult as the road to Olduvai had been. Digging for fossils takes money—for tools, equipment, assistants, food, and supplies—and Mary and Louis didn't have any. So Louis wrote books to earn money, and he gave lectures to get people interested enough in the Leakeys' work to give them money to do it. He also got a job as the head of a museum in Nairobi, Kenya, where they lived when they weren't at Olduvai. Meanwhile, Mary dug whenever they had enough money.

Mary and Louis were very different kinds of people—and scientists. While Louis was happy lecturing, traveling, talking to reporters, and asking for money, Mary wanted to look for fossils and stone tools. While Louis was eager to put forth his theories about how humans evolved, Mary wanted to find the evidence. She worked very hard and found many stone tools. In fact, she uncovered the oldest stone tools ever found. She studied these first tools, and she learned more about choppers and scrapers and flakes than anybody else ever had.

Millions of years ago, the apelike creatures of Africa had made simple tools out of stones. They smashed two stones together to form a sharp edge, or a point, or whatever they needed. They made hand axes and anvils, awls, chisels and choppers. The flakes that flew off were tools, too. They used their tools to skin an animal for its hide, or to cut into it for meat. They used tools to punch holes into the hide. They used them as weapons.

When these apelike creatures began making tools, they started on the path that led to modern human civilization. By examining the different kinds of tools, comparing those from different ages, and even making tools themselves, Mary, Louis, and other scientists could figure out a lot about the creatures who made the tools. They could learn about their hands—what they looked like and how they worked. They could learn what these creatures ate and how they lived. They could begin to get a better picture of how we became human.

But both Mary and Louis kept looking for the ancient creature itself. They kept looking for the bones of our earliest human ancestors. They looked and looked and found next to nothing. But they kept looking.

Louis once said that living in Africa trained them to really notice things, and to be patient. In Africa, he said, "a torn leaf, a paw print, a bush that rustles when there is not a breeze, sudden quiet—these are the signals that spell the difference between life and death. The same instant recognition of something different—a glint of white in the face of a cliff, an odd-shaped pebble, a tiny fragment of bone—leads to the discovery of fossils." In 1948, their hard work and patience began to pay off on a place called Rusinga Island.

If we looked at the artifacts from Mary's life now, we would see sieves, camel-hair brushes, and archaeologist's charts—and mixed in with those tools of archaeology we would see children's toys. For Mary was a mother now, too. Mary and Louis had two sons: Jonathan, born in 1940, and Richard, born in 1944. (An infant daughter had died.)

Mary hired a babysitter to care for the children and brought them with her on excavations whenever possible. So Jonathan and Richard grew up living in the wild—and, for the most part, loving it. Jonathan's

passion was always snakes (and still is, now that he is a grown-up). Richard declared as a child that he would never hunt for fossils, but today he is a world-famous fossil hunter!

In September 1948, Louis and Mary, along with Jonathan, then eight years old, and Richard, four, went to Rusinga Island in Lake Victoria, East Africa, to search for very early human ancestors. Rusinga Island had ape fossils that were about eighteen million years old. Mary and Louis thought they might find remains of another creature, a creature that was in between apes and humans. Scientists called that creature the "missing link." It was still missing.

On the afternoon of October 2, Louis decided to excavate a fossil of an extinct crocodile he had found. Mary had never liked crocodiles—dead or alive—so she went on looking for fossil apes.

She settled down in an area that she and Louis had already explored seven times without success. But on this afternoon Mary saw something. There were pieces of a bone sticking out of the dirt. Slowly she looked up along the slope and saw something else. It was white. It was a tooth. It looked like the tooth of an ancient hominid, a member of the human family. "Louis!" she shouted as loudly as she could. Louis came running. But as excited as they were, he and Mary had to stay calm. Very gently they brushed away the dirt and rocks around the tooth.

They realized immediately that it was the tooth of a *Proconsul*. Remains of *Proconsul* had been found before; some scientists thought that this creature might be the "missing link" between apes and humans. As they carefully brushed away the dirt, they saw that it wasn't just a tooth—it was a tooth in a jaw! Only bits and pieces of *Proconsul* had been found before. This was clearly more than just bits and pieces. Gently, slowly, carefully, over the course of two days, they dug out the fossil.

Back in camp, Mary spent long hours putting together the pieces of what was, it now seemed, part of a skull. There were more than thirty pieces. Once, when she dropped a tiny piece onto the tent floor, she got down on her hands and knees and searched through the dust until she found it. She *had* to find it—it joined two bigger pieces. When she was finally finished, Mary had more than half of a *Proconsul* skull. Before this, scientists could only guess at the size and shape of a hominid skull this old. Now Mary was staring at the humanlike face of a creature that had lived *twenty million* years ago.

When Mary and Louis realized what a wonderful discovery they had made, they decided to celebrate by having another baby! Philip Leakey was born in June 1949. Even though he owed his birth to archaeology, Philip was never very interested in what his parents did.

When he was a child he once angrily told a friend of the Leakeys, "All I get at home is stones and bones!" (He grew up to be a politician in the Kenyan government.)

After Mary pieced the skull together, she put it in a box and flew back to London, holding the box on her knees the whole time. (When she got off the plane for a stopover in Egypt, the pilot locked it in the cockpit.) With police escorts to and from the airport, Mary and the skull attracted worldwide attention! In London, Mary showed the skull to Le Gros Clark, an expert on the anatomy of prehistoric animals. In his report he said it had both hominid and monkey features. Newspaper reporters declared *Proconsul* the "missing link."

Today, actually, scientists are fairly certain that there is no such thing as one missing link. Scientists now think that apes and humans have a common ancestor far back on the family tree. The tree

branched off five million years ago, and that ancestor evolved into different creatures that led to great apes, other primates, and modern human beings.

Thirty years after Mary found *Proconsul*, scientists found missing pieces of the skull, and with those they were able to piece together an even better picture. They decided that *Proconsul* was indeed a very early ancestor of chimpanzees, gibbons, orangutans, gorillas—and modern humans.

After all the attention *Proconsul* received, Mary was eager to get back to Olduvai Gorge to see what she could find next. In the meantime she received money to study some rock paintings made by late

Stone Age people. In the Kondoa region of Tanganyika, Mary and her team traced sixteen hundred figures in three months. (Once, the wind blew away their tracings, and they had to start all over!)

Mary felt it was very important to trace these paintings because they were being ruined by time, weather, and people. Tourists would throw water on the rocks to make the colors brighter, just as you do with a pebble on the beach. But the water was fading the ancient paint. At first it was very difficult to see what was in the pictures because there were paintings on top of one another. But with concentration, Mary could see the different paintings and could learn about parts of Stone Age life that she couldn't know from stones and bones. She saw pictures of people hunting, dancing, singing, and playing music. She was able to see different hairstyles—some figures had long hair, with braids and feathers. She noticed jewelry—armbands, body bands, and necklaces. She saw black rhinos and white rhinos, zebras, giraffes, ostriches, and snakes. And she noticed that even then people kept dogs.

In 1951 Mary and Louis took a wealthy British man named Charles Boise to see the rock paintings and to visit Olduvai. Boise was so impressed with their work that he gave them enough money to dig at Olduvai for seven years. Finally, Mary could do what she had been wanting to do since she first set foot there in 1935. She could plan long, detailed research at the most promising prehistoric site in East Africa.

CHAPTER 7

"Oh, You Dear Boy!"

Mary Leakey was an exacting scientist and a tough boss. She would not tolerate messy, haphazard digging, and she often lost her temper at workers who were not good enough. In fact, she introduced the way of working that all archaeologists in Africa now use. Before Mary Leakey, archaeologists in Africa dug deep holes, so they could see how the earth, and fossils in it, changed over time. But Mary thought it was better to dig in shallow layers, so she could study the fossil bones and tools along with the earth of their time.

Every tool or fossil, no matter how little, had to be charted so Mary knew exactly where it had been found. Knowing exactly where a fossil or stone tool was buried is very important. A friend of Mary's, the geologist Richard Hay, figured out that the gorge was divided into layers of different ages. He labeled these layers, or "beds." By figuring out how old a layer of volcanic ash is, scientists can tell how old the bones are that are buried in that layer.

There are different methods of dating fossils using the earth in which they are found. One method, called potassium/argon dating, was developed in the 1950s and was used at Olduvai. Potassium is an element that is found in many places on Earth (including our bodies).

When a volcano is born, the potassium is pure. When the volcano erupts, the potassium begins to decay. It continues to decay as the volcanic rock sits around for years and years. As the potassium decays, it builds up a gas called argon. The more argon there is in the rock, the older the rock is. Since Olduvai Gorge is filled with volcanic rock, it was a good place to use potassium/argon dating.

Mary, Louis, and their assistants found more than two thousand stone tools, and many fossilized mammal bones. They found a giant pig, the size of a modern hippopotamus, and a baboon the size of a gorilla. But with all of their searching, they didn't find what they were really looking for. They didn't find the ancient prehuman who lived in Olduvai.

Until. . .

One morning in July 1959, Louis was lying in bed sick with the flu. Mary was in the gorge, searching through rubble, which is called scree. She had brought along her Dalmatians Sally and Victoria for company. At about noon, she decided to go back to camp to join Louis for some lunch. She stood up carefully, for it is easy to slip on a scree slope. Suddenly, she spotted a couple of teeth sticking out of the scree. Mary bent down and, with a soft camel-hair brush, dusted the surface. She knew immediately that she had found hominid teeth. And she could see that there was much more of the creature in the ground. Finally, after twenty-five years! "Oh, you dear boy!" Mary cried.

She marked the spot and raced back to camp in her Land Rover. It took Mary fifteen minutes to drive up the winding track out of the gorge and onto the shoulders of the canyon to get back to camp. It must have seemed like an eternity.

She ran into the tent where Louis was sleeping feverishly. "I've got him," she said. "I've got him."

"Got what, Mary?" asked Louis.

"I've got the man! I've got the man!"

Louis forgot about his flu and they raced back to the gorge to look at "Dear Boy."

By coincidence there was a team of filmmakers due to arrive the next day, to make a film of the Leakeys at work. So although Mary and Louis wanted to begin digging right away, they decided to wait for the filmmakers. They left the fossil in the ground, covered carefully by a pile of stones. One of their African assistants stood guard all night.

The next day, when the filmmakers arrived, Mary and Louis started digging up Dear Boy. With the cameras rolling, they slowly and carefully removed the many pieces of bone. They removed two teeth in

the upper jaw. They removed more pieces of the jaw, pieces of the palate, pieces of the cranium . . . It was the first time that anything like that had been excavated in front of a movie camera. It took nineteen days to remove the pieces of the skull from its resting spot in the earth. After all of the big pieces were excavated, they searched the rest of the nearby dirt with a sieve that looks like a window screen. They found many more pieces.

Back in camp, Mary began to piece together the skull—all four hundred pieces of it! It took her eighteen months. But before she put it all together, Louis was eager to know what she had found. So a few weeks after they dug up all the pieces, Mary, again with the fossil in a box on her lap, flew with Louis to Johannesburg, South Africa, to compare Dear Boy with some South African hominid fossils. There they showed their find to Raymond Dart, the scientist who had found the first ape-man fossil in South Africa in the 1920s, and Phillip Tobias, a physical anthropologist.

"It was the most marvelous specimen!" Tobias remembers. But Mary hung in the background while Louis showed off the fossil.

Dart turned to Louis and said, "I am so happy, Louis, that this has happened to you."

Tobias was upset on Mary's behalf. "Mary was in many ways a better scientist than Louis," he says. "She was prepared to collect the facts, the fossil facts from the earth, the hard facts of human evolution, while he presented them on platforms and on television."

What exactly had Mary found? It was a creature, probably a male, a teenager when he died one and three-quarter million years ago. What kind of creature was he? He was clearly an apelike creature, with some human features. Did he make tools? Did he walk on two feet? Was it his kind that evolved into human beings? In the field of pre-history, just finding the fossils is difficult enough. But deciding what those fossils are—and getting your fellow scientists to agree with you—is often more difficult. Mary herself preferred to find the fossils and piece them together, without rushing to name them. Louis was always willing—and eager—to say where he thought the fossils fit into the big picture of human evolution. Like many other paleoanthropologists, he wanted to find the earliest direct ancestor of human beings. He wanted to find—and name—the creature that evolved into modern people.

Louis decided Dear Boy was of a new genus, a whole new kind, of ancient prehuman creature. He named it *Zinjanthropus boisei*. Zinjanthropus means "man of East Africa." Boisei comes from Charles Boise, the man who gave Mary and Louis money to excavate at Olduvai.

Mary and Louis asked Tobias to do a detailed study of the skull. He came to the conclusion that it wasn't of a new genus. He decided it was just a new species of a genus called *Australopithecus*, an "apeman." Other species of *Australopithecus* had been found in South Africa. This one was more robust than any others that had been found. He had huge molars, which Tobias called "a monumental set of nutcrackers," so newspapers nicknamed him Nutcracker Man. The huge molars were probably used to chew a lot of tough, stringy plants and nuts. He was also known by many as Zinj. By 1967, he was officially renamed *Australopithecus boisei*, as Phillip Tobias had suggested. To Mary Leakey, he was always "Dear Boy."

And what a dear boy he was for the Leakey family! He captured the imagination of people all over the world as the "earliest man," bringing Mary and Louis more publicity, and more money for research, than they had ever dreamed of having. The National Geographic Society funded their work and featured them regularly in *National Geographic* magazine. In 1962 Mary and Louis went to Washington, D.C., to receive the gold Hubbard Award from the National Geographic Society, the first of many awards for both of them. Because of Dear Boy, the name Leakey was forever linked with the search for human origins.

CHAPTER 8

A New Path

The 1960s were very busy for Mary Leakey and her family. In many ways they were good years, but they were difficult also. The Leakeys and their team found more exciting fossils at Olduvai. The Leakeys' son Jonathan, then twenty, found one that Louis named *Homo habilis*, which means "Handy Man." Louis thought this was the species that made the tools at Olduvai. He decided that *Homo habilis*, not Zinj, was the ancestor of humans.

If we looked for artifacts from Mary's life at Olduvai at this time, we might find bottles of wine that were served to the many visitors, leftovers of big meals, including delicious homemade bread, tourists' cameras, and reporters' notebooks. We would also find evidence of many animals, both wild and tame, who were living at Olduvai.

Mary, of course, had her Dalmatians, sometimes as many as four or five at a time. And she had other pets—most unusual ones, both there and back at their house in Nairobi. She had a pet wildebeest calf who liked to barge into tents while women were bathing. She had a Sykes monkey named Simon, who could have been the model for Curious George, he was so naughty.

One night Simon broke into the liquor cabinet. The next morning Mary found him lying face down, unconscious, in a puddle of alcohol.

Simon then went to live in an animal orphanage, where he settled down happily with a female monkey.

Mary also had pet snakes (they were really Jonathan's, but Mary ended up in charge of them while Jonathan was away at boarding school) and a pet owl, for whom she kept minced rat meat in the refrigerator. Visitors to their house in Nairobi were often surprised by a rock hyrax jumping on them from behind.

While Mary stayed in Nairobi or at Olduvai, Louis traveled the world over getting money and getting publicity—and getting into arguments with other prehistorians.

Eventually Mary and Louis got into some professional arguments themselves. Those arguments added to personal problems they were already having, and their marriage began to fall apart. By 1968 Mary and Louis were living separate lives, although they did not take any official steps to end their marriage. With her son Richard's help, Mary set up a permanent camp at Olduvai, with metal huts for sleeping, eating, and working. There was even an airstrip now.

In 1972 Louis, Mary, and Richard had a visit together and, in Mary's words, it was like old times. Richard was now a fossil hunter himself, and Mary and Louis were delighted with the find he had just made of a *Homo habilis* skull. They spent a very happy evening together in their house in Nairobi. The next day Richard drove Louis to the airport, where he flew off to London, more content than Mary had seen him in a long time.

A few days later, while Mary was in camp at Olduvai, she heard a small plane flying low overhead. Her son Philip had come with bad news: Louis Leakey had died of a heart attack that morning in London.

Mary made arrangements for Louis's funeral and memorial service, and took care of financial arrangements that had to be made. But by the time Louis died, Mary had her own life at Olduvai, and she was eager to get back. And she still had a secret to uncover at Laetoli, the site she had visited on her very first trip to Africa.

In 1975, forty years after she first visited there, Mary went back to Laetoli. She and her staff uncovered very old fossils and some fossilized animal tracks, including those of rhinoceroses, insects, birds, and elephants. In 1976 Mary's son Philip and a scientist named Peter Jones even found what they thought might be hominid footprints. But the footprints were not clear enough to say for sure.

Then, one day in 1978, Paul Abell, a scientist who was excavating a block of rhino footprints, was walking around with the geologist Richard Hay. All of a sudden Abell stopped. "Look at that, Dick," he said. "That looks like a hominid footprint." He went to get Mary.

Although she was recovering from a broken ankle, Mary knew this was something she had to see. When Mary saw the footprint, so clearly made by a hominid, she decided to excavate it and look for more. Before, when she had found *Proconsul* and Dear Boy, Mary knew almost right away that she had found something terrific. This time, the grandeur of the find appeared gradually. But over the next two field seasons Mary Leakey and her staff uncovered the most exciting find of her career: It was a trail of hominid footprints, more than three and a half million years old!

The footprints were made by three short hominids walking together—perhaps a male, a female, and a child. It looks as though the child was playing Follow the Leader, because the small footprints are inside the larger ones. These footprints are the earliest physical evidence of bipedalism. Scientists believe that hominids started walking

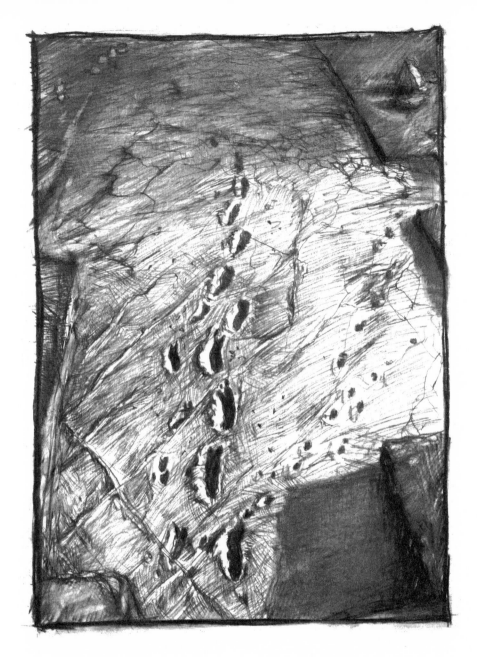

on two feet five million years ago. When those ancient creatures rose up on two feet, they started on the path that separated them from their ape cousins. They started on the path that led to modern human beings.

"The slanting light of evening throws the hominid prints into sharp relief," Mary wrote in *National Geographic* magazine, "so sharp that they could have been left this morning. I cannot help but think about the distant creatures who made them. Where did they come from? Where were they going? . . . Across the gulf of time I can only wish them well on that prehistoric trek."

The footprints not only shed light on those early human ancestors, but they also cast the spotlight on Mary Leakey. Finally, she was famous in her own right, out from Louis's shadow. Now the world knew what those who worked with her had known all along—what a superb scientist Mary Leakey was. Someone once said that Mary had found all of Louis's greatest finds. Another said, "Mary was Louis Leakey's greatest find!" In 1978 Mary Leakey was the first woman to receive the Swedish Golden Linnaeus Medal, a very high honor, in recognition of her contribution to the biological sciences. That was just one of many honors she won. She also received honorary degrees from the University of Witwatersrand in South Africa, Yale in the United States, and Oxford in England. Finally she could add college diplomas to her collection of artifacts!

In 1982 Mary became blind in one eye. Unable to see well enough to excavate, she moved back to her house in Nairobi. Now she lives surrounded by her father's paintings and her Dalmatians. She enjoys visits with her sons and grandchildren, and her friends, with whom she shares a good drink—and a good cigar! She hasn't retired, though. She has published a beautiful book about the rock paintings in Kondoa with Richard's wife, Meave. In 1984 she wrote her autobiography. And she is still writing scientific articles and books about her many finds at Olduvai.

No matter how much—or how little—we find out about our early beginnings in years to come, we will always be indebted to Mary Leakey for the evidence she uncovered. Because of *Proconsul*, the rock paintings, Dear Boy, the stone tools, and the footprints at Laetoli, we can walk alongside our earliest ancestors on their prehistoric journey. We can walk with them on the journey from their world to ours.

INDEX/GLOSSARY

INDEX/GLOSSARY

INDEX/GLOSSARY

FURTHER READING AND VIEWING

To find out more about Mary Leakey and her family—and to learn more about early humans, prehistoric times, and archaeology—look for more books at your library or bookstore. Here are a few books to get you started.

Dig This! How Archaeologists Uncover Our Past by Michael Avi-Yonah

(Minneapolis, Minnesota: Runestone Press, 1993.) Although this book describes archaeological work of more recent sites, mostly in the Middle East, it will give you a good idea of the life and work of an archaeologist.

The Encyclopedia of Evolution by Richard Milner

(New York: Facts On File, 1990.) This is a one-volume encyclopedia that has entries on all aspects of evolution. Like any of these books, some of the facts are already out of date as scientists are continually discovering new things.

The Leakey Family: Leaders in the Search for Human Origins by Delta Willis

(New York: Facts On File, 1992.) This book discusses the work of Louis, Richard, and Meave Leakey as well as Mary Leakey.

The Leakeys by Lisa A. Lambert

(Vero Beach, Florida: Rourke Publications, 1993.) This book also discusses the entire Leakey family.

Lucy's Child by Donald Johanson and James Shreeve

(New York: William Morrow, 1989.) This is a book for adults, but it is wonderfully written and has wonderful descriptions of Olduvai Gorge and the work done there as well as other spots in Africa by one of the Leakeys' rivals, Donald Johanson.

Traces of Life: The Origins of Humankind by Kathryn Lasky

(New York: Morrow Junior Books, 1989.) A good look at the history of hominid research and the paleoanthropologists who do the work. Includes the Leakeys as well as their rivals. Beautiful illustrations.

The World Book Encyclopedia

This widely available set has very good information under the heading "Prehistoric People."

The Making of Mankind

(BBC) This is an excellent video series about human evolution and the scientists who study it. The second video in the series is called "One Small Step. . ." It is about Mary Leakey's discovery of the footprints at Laetoli. Check out the video section in your library for other videos about the Leakeys.